FANTASTIC FACTS ABOUT

BIRDS & FISH

Author
Martin Walters

Editor
Steve Parker

Design
Pentacor

Image Co-ordination
Ian Paulyn

Production Assistant
Rachel Jones

Index
Janet de Saulles

Editorial Director
Paula Borton

Design Director
Clare Sleven

Publishing Director
Jim Miles

This is a Parragon Book
First published in 2000

Parragon, Queen Street House, 4 Queen Street, Bath, BA1 1HE, UK

Copyright © Parragon 2000

Parragon has previously printed this material in 1999 as part of the Factfinder series

2 4 6 8 10 9 7 5 3 1

Produced by Miles Kelly Publishing Ltd
Bardfield Centre, Great Bardfield, Essex CM7 4SL

ISBN 0-75253-387-8

Printed in Italy Milanostampa Caleppio Milano

FANTASTIC FACTS ABOUT

BIRDS & FISH

p

CONTENTS

INTRODUCTION

Birds are some of the most colourful, noisy and conspicuous members of the animal kingdom. Almost wherever water occurs in nature you will find fish — whether it's in a cold mountain stream, a warm tropical lake, or in the oceans. Here you will encounter hundreds of different kinds of birds and fish and find out how we can help to preserve some of our endangered species.

BIRDS AND FISH is a handy reference guide in the *Fascinating Facts* series. Each book has been specially compiled with a collection of stunning illustrations and photographs which bring the subject to life. Hundreds of facts and figures are presented in a variety of interesting ways and side-panels provide information at-a-glance. This unique combination is fun and easy to use and makes learning a pleasure.

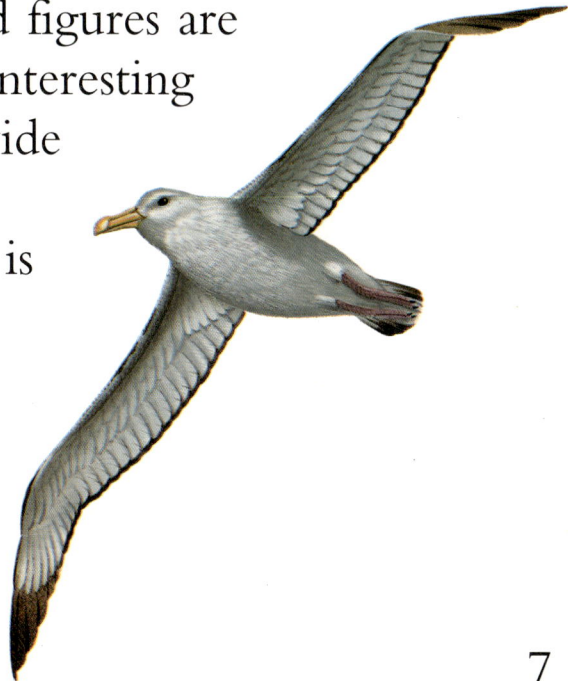

BIRDS

Active mainly by 'day, conspicuous, and often colourful and noisy, birds are well-known to everyone. Many birds announce their presence by loud calls or musical songs. There are some 9,000 kinds or species of birds around the world, in all land habitats, and also on water and at sea.

Birds are the most prominent animals in many of the world's ecosystems, from the polar regions to the tropics. This is partly because their powers of flight gives them extra mobility. Even the Arctic wastes thrill to bird song during the busy breeding season.

THE UNIQUE FEATHER

Birds are warm-blooded and insulated by their feathers, which are their unique feature. So birds can be active even under cool or cold conditions.

As well as keeping birds warm, feathers play a vital part in flying. The main flight feathers rest in sockets in the wing bones. The number of feathers a bird has depends on its species, size and sex.

BIRDS EVERYWHERE

Since birds lay hard-shelled eggs they do not need to depend on water for breeding, and this has helped birds to colonize most regions, even isolated oceanic islands.

FLIGHTLESS BIRDS

The best-known flightless birds are probably the ostrich, which lives on the African plains, and the emu of Australia. The cassowary is another flightless bird from Australia, while the rhea dwells in South America. All of these birds can run fast and use their powerful legs and bills (beaks) against predators.

The chicken-sized kiwis of New Zealand are another flightless group. They have fluffy, fur-like feathers and tiny wings.

FLYING UNDER WATER
The largest group of flightless birds is the penguins, from the Southern Hemisphere. Their wings are like tough paddles. Penguins flap their wings when submerged to achieve a sort of underwater flight.

LOST THE POWER OF FLIGHT

In addition to these groups of flightless birds, there are some members of flying groups which have lost the power of flight. Flightless rails are found on certain isolated islands. New Zealand has a flightless parrot, the kakapo, which hides under rocks and undergrowth by day and emerges at night to feed.

Wings

Male ostrich

EMPEROR PENGUINS

Most penguins live on rocky islands, the icy shores of mainland Antarctica, or on drifting icebergs and ice floes. They catch fish, squid, shrimps, krill and other sea animals for food. The emperor is the largest penguin, about 120 centimetres tall.

Birds (Aves)
9,000 species
• possess feathers
• lay hard-shelled eggs
• scaly legs
• front limbs are wings
• beak without teeth
• warm-blooded

Flightless birds include:

Ostriches
1 species
• Africa

Emus
1 species
• Australia

Rheas
2 species
• South America

Cassowaries
3 species
• Australia, New Guinea

Kiwis
3 species
• New Zealand

Penguins
16 species
• Antarctic region and southern oceans

11

SEA BIRDS

Many different kinds of bird have become adapted to life at sea. Best known are the gulls and terns, hardly ever absent from a visit to the coast or on a boat trip. Gulls are equally at home far inland, and often feed on open fields, especially in the winter. Terns are graceful sea birds, which catch their fish prey by darting, near-vertical dives.

The real expert ocean-goers are the albatrosses and petrels, which spend weeks far out at sea. Albatrosses save energy by gliding on up-currents from the waves as they cross the oceans. Very different in build, but nevertheless well-adapted for life at sea are the auks. Their plump bodies and tight feathering insulate them well, and they are also adept divers.

Wandering albatross

STORM PETREL
The only time this bird alights on land is during the breeding season, on remote islands or outcrops.

Long, slim, narrow wings adapted for gliding and soaring

Primary (wing-tip) feathers

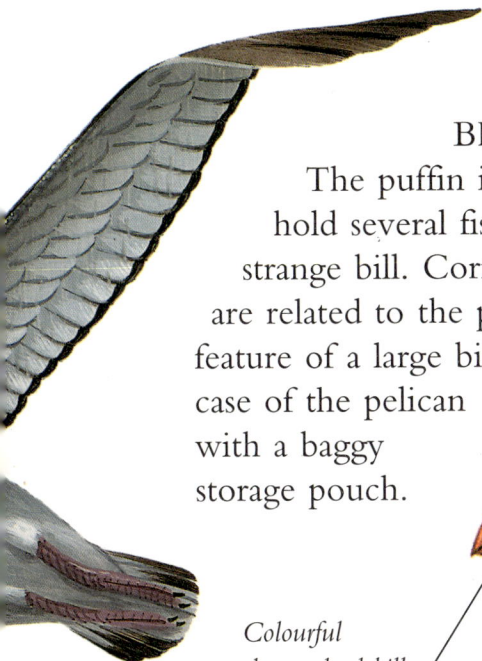

BIG BILLS

The puffin is an auk and can hold several fish at once in its strange bill. Cormorants and pelicans are related to the puffin and share the feature of a large bill, equipped in the case of the pelican with a baggy storage pouch.

Colourful sharp-edged bill grasps slippery food

Legs pack under body, for good swimming

Webbed feet

PUFFIN

Most auks are colonial breeders, and their nest sites are noisy and filled with activity. The puffin's bright bill becomes even more colourful during the breeding season, to attract and court a mate. Puffins nest in burrows in clifftop soil, including old rabbit warrens. These birds catch small fish such as sand-eels, and also shellfish and worms.

Main groups of seabirds include:

Gulls and terns
95 species
• mostly white or grey
• narrow wings

Albatrosses, petrels
93 species
• ocean seabirds
• long, narrow wings

Pelicans, cormorants, gannets
57 species
• gliding and soaring flight
• white or very dark plumage
• feet completely webbed (all four toes)
• throat pouch

Auks
22 species
• compact and dumpy body
• dive well
• mainly black and white plumage

WATERFOWL

Water-birds are built primarily for swimming. They have buoyant bodies and webbed or lobed feet to help push themselves through the water. Many, notably the geese and swans, have long, flexible necks which they can use to reach down into the water as they feed.

Bar-headed goose

SWAN

Swans pair for life, male and female staying together until one dies. They feed in shallow water on weeds, stems and leaves. Baby swans are called cygnets.

WHITE AND BLACK

The swans are the largest water-birds and most have pure white plumage. An exception is the Australian black swan, which is mostly black, with a bright red bill. Ducks tend either to be surface feeders, like the mallard, or divers, such as the pochard and tufted duck. Ducks and geese are powerful in flight and can reach speeds of up to 90 kilometres per hour. They also fly high when migrating. The bar-headed goose, for example, has been seen at 9,000 metres when flying over the Himalayan Mountains.

GREBES AND DIVERS

Grebes are more delicate water-birds. They build floating nests on lakes and ponds, and have lobed rather than webbed feet.

Divers (or loons) are streamlined water-birds which spend most of their time on lakes or at sea. They are very clumsy on land as their legs are set far back on their bodies, perfect for swimming but not for walking!

Small head for size

Ragged crest

HOATZIN

This strange bird spends most of its life clambering in the branches of trees along riverbanks and swamps in South America. It is a poor flier, and although regarded as a water-bird, it is more closely related to cuckoos and gamebirds than to swans and ducks. The young hoatzin has a pair of claws on the front of each wing, to help it climb in trees. These are an evolutionary left-over from ancient times. The claws are lost as the hoatzin grows.

Large-clawed feet hold twigs

Main groups of water-birds include:

Ducks, geese, swans
150 species
- most are good swimmers
- webbed feet
- many species are long-necked
- bill usually flattened and quite short

Grebes
20 species
- very good swimmers and divers
- worldwide
- lobed feet

Divers or loons
4 species
- water-birds, very good swimmers and divers
- breed in or near the Arctic

WADING BIRDS

Birds that wade include herons and storks, and the true waders such as curlews and avocets.

There are about 60 different species of herons found throughout the temperate and tropical parts of the world. A heron feeds by waiting until a frog or fish gets into range, then stabbing suddenly down to catch the prey in its long bill. Long legs help herons, storks and flamingos feed in quite deep water, without having to swim.

TRUE WADERS

Waders can be found at the water's edge, either at the muddy margins of lakes and ponds, or more typically flocking to the seashore. They feed by probing into soft soil or mud for insects, crustaceans, worms

Broad feet do not sink in soft mud

Spear-shaped bill darts at fish and frogs

SANDHILL CRANE
There are 15 kinds of cranes. Most are rare and protected by wildlife laws. They live in flocks except during the breeding season, when they pair off and carry out elaborate, noisy courtship dances.

GREEN-BACKED HERON

This small type of heron waits motionless on an overhanging branch for prey in the water below.

and other small creatures. Plovers, sandpipers, oystercatchers and curlews are all in this group. Curlews use their long, curved bills to extract worms and larvae from deep below the surface. The bill of the oyster-catcher is used like a chisel to prise apart the shells of molluscs such as mussels and oysters.

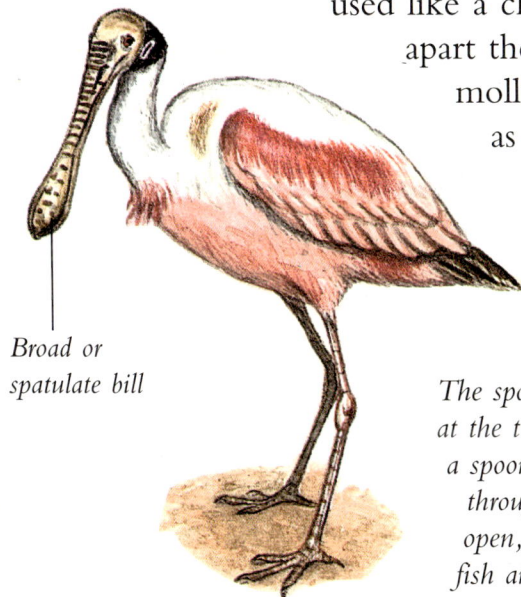

Broad or spatulate bill

SPOONBILL

The spoonbill's beak widens at the tip, but is not used as a spoon. Instead, it swishes through the water, slightly open, to sieve out small fish and other creatures.

Main groups of wading birds include:

Herons, storks, ibises, flamingos

115 species

• most are freshwater wetland birds
• long legs, long neck, large bill
• most species are large

True waders

200 species

• most are freshwater wetland or seashore birds
• long legs, many have long bill
• medium-sized or small
• some feed in large groups

OWLS

Owls, nightjars and frogmouths are specialist night-hunters.

Owls can fly silently and also quite slowly. The soft edging to their feathers helps to cut down the sound of their wings moving through the air. Although they have good vision in the dusk, owls mainly detect their prey on the darkest night by hearing. They can hear four times better than a cat. The smaller owls mostly eat insects and other invertebrates; the larger species take small birds and small mammals.

FISHY FOOD

The fishing owls of Africa and Asia feed on fish and amphibians. These owls have long, unfeathered legs and very sharp claws to grab prey as they swoop over the surface.

SNOWY OWL
Most owls have brown, mottled or striped plumage, but the snowy owl is pure white (adult male) or white with dark barring (adult female). This makes the snowy owl hard to see in its snowy Arctic habitat.

NIGHTJARS

Nightjars look like overgrown swallows in shape. But they have patterned brown plumage for excellent camouflage. This makes them almost impossible to spot as they sit among leaves and twigs by day. At night they flit about, snapping up moths in their huge mouths. Some nightjars have long, thin, whisker-like feathers around their mouths, to feel for prey in the darkness.

Feathers form facial disc that channels sounds into ears

TAWNY OWL
The tawny is one of the most common owls and lives across Europe, North Africa and northern Asia. Like most owls, it hunts small creatures such as mice, voles, baby rabbits and small birds. When food is short it also preys on beetles and worms.

Owls
135 species
- most are nocturnal
- soft feathers
- large, flat face and large eyes
- camouflaged plumage

Nightjars and frogmouths
100 species
- nocturnal
- sleek and graceful
- large, dark eyes
- large gape
- camouflaged plumage

Owl records
- The barn owl has the widest distribution of any bird, being found in every continent except Antarctica, and across many different climates and habitats.
- The tiny elf-owl from the southern USA and Mexico measures only about 12 centimetres in height.
- The largest owl is the European eagle owl, which can measure 70 centimetres tall, with a wingspan of 150 centimetres.

BIRDS OF PREY

There are some 295 species of bird of prey (apart from owls), found throughout the world. They range in size from tiny falconets, almost as small as sparrows, to the massive condors, vultures and sea eagles.

Birds of prey share the features of powerful talons with sharp claws for grasping their prey, a sharp, hooked beak for tearing at flesh, and large eyes giving amazing vision. Many of the smaller birds of prey eat insects, while some, such as the osprey and fish eagles, rely mostly on fish.

THE FASTEST FLIERS

These aerial predators, also called raptors, include some of the world's most acrobatic and speedy fliers. Certain falcons, notably the hobbies and peregrine, are adapted to chase and catch other birds in swift flight. They can twist and turn faster than our eyes can follow.

Long, pointed wings for aerobatic manoeuvres

Hooked bill for tearing up victim

PEREGRINE

One of the largest falcons, the peregrine is unequalled in the speed and precision of its flight. It lives in various habitats, usually remote mountains and uplands. The 17 various geographic groups show different plumage, especially in the speckles and bars on the chest.

SPARROWHAWK
As well as sparrows, this woodland predator catches tits and many other small birds. Like many birds of prey, the female is slightly larger than the male.

Bright yellow legs

NOT BALD
One of the most impressive raptors is the bald eagle – which is not bald at all. Its white-feathered head appears naked from a distance. This species is the national bird of the USA. It is a kind of fish eagle.

MARTIAL EAGLE
The eagles are the largest raptors and take prey up to the size of hares, small deer. and sometimes farm animals such as young lambs.

Birds of prey groups include:

American vultures
7 species
• large
• powerful bill, naked head
• soaring flight

Secretary bird
1 species
• lives on African grasslands
• long legs and crest
• eats reptiles, especially lizards and snakes

Osprey
1 species
• worldwide
• hunts fish

Falcons and relatives
62 species
• worldwide
• small to medium-sized
• long tail

Hawks, eagles, buzzards, vultures and relatives
224 species
• worldwide
• medium-sized to large
• hunt live prey

PHEASANTS AND PIGEONS

Pheasants are long-tailed members of the gamebird group, or galliforms. Male pheasants are beautifully coloured and patterned, in shades of blue, red and gold, but the females have drab, camouflaged plumage. This is because the male's main job is to impress and court the female, at breeding time. But afterwards, the female's main task is to raise the chicks while sitting on the nest. So camouflage is very important in these generally woodland or forest birds.

TASTY MEAT

Grouse, turkeys, partridges, quails and guinea fowl also belong to this group. Many of these are hunted, by other animals as well as people, since they are plump and their meat is very tasty. Doves and pigeons are well-known for their soothing calls, and from the tame pigeons which flock in the squares of many towns and cities.

Male monal pheasant in bright breeding plumage

MONAL PHEASANT

Most pheasants and other gamebirds have stout, heavy bodies and spend much time on the ground searching for plant food. They fly fast and low with rapid, whirring wingbeats, but have little stamina for travelling long distances.

Strong legs and feet for walking and running

The European cuckoo is the best known of all the cuckoos, but there are more than 125 other kinds around the world. About one-third are brood-parasites. They lay their eggs in the nest of another species and let the unrelated host do all the hard work of rearing the cuckoo's chick.

Soft colours give good camouflage

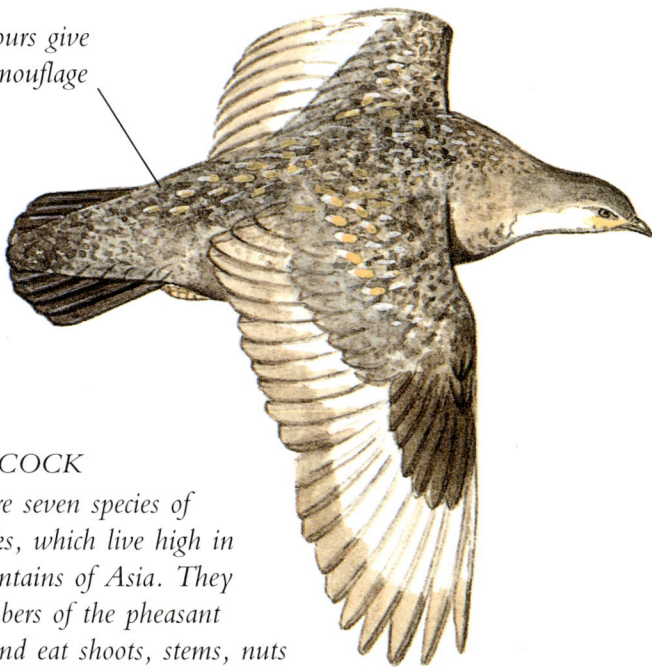

SNOWCOCK
There are seven species of snowcocks, which live high in the mountains of Asia. They are members of the pheasant family and eat shoots, stems, nuts and berries. They can withstand extremely low temperatures as they rest at night. By day they walk and fly short distances along the slopes, searching for soft new plant-matter.

Gamebirds and similar groups include:

Gamebirds
260 species

Pigeons, doves
300 species

Cuckoos and relatives
150 species

Sandgrouse
16 species

Sandgrouse are grouse-like birds of dry desert habitats.

• The males bring drinking water to the chicks by soaking their breast feathers at a water-hole and then flying back to the nest.

• The round journey to collect moisture like this from the nearest water-hole or oasis may be more than 50 kilometres.

23

PARROTS

Parrots are comical-looking birds with heavy, often hooked bills, and an inquisitive expression and nature. They are intelligent and long-lived, which goes some way towards explaining their popularity as cage-birds. Only cage-bred birds should be kept, however, and many parrots die each year during illegal smuggling. Several kinds of parrot are highly endangered in the wild.

CRUSHED NUTS

The bill of a parrot can crush even the heaviest seeds and nuts. But is also used as a kind of third limb, to help the parrot clamber about through the branches of trees.

BUDGIE

The budgerigar is a small species of parrot, native to Australia. Cage-bred budgies come in many colours, but wild budgies are green, and blend in well with the trees and grasses.

GREY PARROT
In the wild, the short, hooked bill is used to open nuts.

In fact, parrots often prefer to climb rather than fly. They use their strong feet to manipulate their food, as well as for perching and climbing. They also taste and manipulate food items with their long, flexible tongue. Although they mimic sounds in captivity, they are rarely known to do so in the wild.

LIFE IN TREES

Most parrots spend almost all their lives in trees, nesting in holes in tree trunks. They rarely land on the ground or fly long distances except to new feeding grounds.

SCARLET MACAW
This is one of the largest and most brightly-coloured members of the parrot group, Psittaciformes. However, it has become rare in the wild, due to its capture for the illegal cage-bird trade, and to the destruction of its rainforest homes in Central and South America.

Parrots, cockatoos and lories

330 species
- chunky birds
- heavy, strong bill
- feet with 2 clawed toes forward and 2 backwards
- mainly green, although some are brightly coloured
- mainly tropical or Southern Hemisphere

The cleverest birds?

- Some tame parrots have been taught to identify and ask for (or refuse) more than 50 different objects. They can almost converse with their trainers!
- Parrots are among the longest-lived birds. Ages of 40-50 years are not unusual and some have lived for 80 years or more.
- The flightless kakapo of New Zealand is actually a kind of parrot. So is New Zealand's kea, which lives in upland country 2,000 metres high, even in snowy weather.

WOODPECKERS

As their name suggests, woodpeckers use their large, sharp, powerful bills to dig into the trunks of trees. They do this to search for insect food such as beetles and grubs under the bark or in the wood, to excavate nesting holes, and to signal to other woodpeckers.

TROPICAL TOUCANS

The toucans of South and Central America are tropical relatives of woodpeckers, best known for their massive, brightly-coloured bills.

Kingfishers are also relatives of woodpeckers. They feed on fish, of course, but some of them take insects and reptiles too. Many have bright plumage and darting flight.

Bee-eaters, another related group, are also bright and long-billed. Their agile flight helps them chase and catch flying insects, including bees, wasps and even hornets, which they then rub on a perch to remove the sting before swallowing.

Bill is made of spongy horn and is very light

TOCO TOUCAN

This South American toucan's huge bill is used for feeding on fruit. It also serves as a bright breeding signal, like a highly coloured flag, to attract mates in the gloom of the rainforest.

*FEMALE GREAT
SPOTTED
WOODPECKER*
*The most common
woodpecker across much
of Europe, this species
also ranges through North
Africa and Asia. The male
has a red patch on the back
of its head.*

*Carmine
bee-eater*

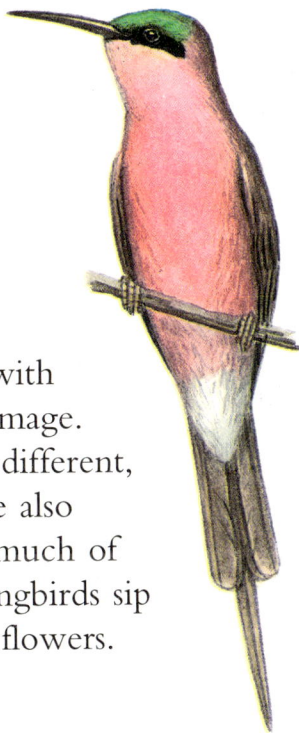

HORNBILLS
The hornbills of Africa and
Asia have large bills, like
toucans, and most feed on
fruit. They are bulky birds with
striking black and white plumage.

Although they look very different,
swifts and hummingbirds are also
related. Both groups spend much of
their lives in flight. Hummingbirds sip
nectar by hovering close to flowers.

Woodpeckers and similar bird
groups include:

True woodpeckers
200 species
• range from sparrow-sized to
crow-sized
Toucans
38 species
Barbets
78 species
Honeyguides
15 species
Kingfishers
86 species
Bee-eaters
24 species
Hornbills
45 species
Rollers
16 species
Swifts
74 species
Hummingbirds
315 species

27

LARGE PERCHING BIRDS

Many birds perch. However, 'perching birds' is also the common name for the huge bird group correctly called the passerines. This group contains about three-fifths of the 9,000 bird species.

These types are known as perching birds because their feet are supremely adapted to clinging onto a perch, such as a twig or branch. Three toes point forwards and one backwards. (In many other birds, two toes point forwards and two back).

CROWS

Larger perching birds include members of the crow family, such as crows, jackdaws, magpies, jays and the very large ravens. Most crows have black or drab plumage, but the jays and magpies are quite colourful. Other larger perching birds are bulbuls, starlings and mynahs, lyrebirds and orioles.

EUROPEAN JAY
The jay, like other crows, has a selection of raucous, hoarse calls. It is an opportunist, eating many foods, from seeds to beetles.

Head crest

BIRDS FROM PARADISE

Perhaps the most spectacular of all the larger perching birds are the birds of paradise. The males are adorned with amazing plumes and colourful feathers. They perform elaborate dances in their Southeast Asian rainforest homes, to attract the females during the breeding season.

WHITE-CHEEKED BULBUL
The many species of bulbul range across Africa and southern Asia.

Adaptable bill can deal with most foods

HILL MYNAH
A noisy and sociable bird, the hill mynah has yellow flaps of skin called wattles on its head. It came originally from southern and Southeast Asia but has been introduced into other regions.

Some of the groups of larger perching birds:

Bulbuls
118 species

Crows, rooks, jays, jackdaws and ravens
116 species

Starlings and mynahs
106 species

Shrikes
70 species

Birds of paradise
43 species

Mockingbirds
30 species

Orioles
28 species

Drongos
20 species

Bowerbirds
18 species

Lyrebirds
2 species

SMALL PERCHING BIRDS

Many of the small, familiar birds of gardens, parks and woodlands around the world belong to the passerine (perching bird) group. They include species such as wrens, tits, finches, sparrows, larks, buntings and swallows.

This group also includes some of the finest songbirds, such as the song thrush and other thrushes, the famous nightingale, and the many different kinds of warbler.

Buntings are finch-like seed-eating birds, often with brightly-coloured plumage. In contrast, many warblers have very drab plumage – shades of yellow, green and brown – which makes them hard to spot. They announce their presence with their loud, pleasant songs and are a major feature of the soundscapes in temperate lands during spring and summer. Indeed, warblers are much more likely to be heard than seen, and some species are identified most easily by their songs – they are so similar in appearance!

THE SMALLEST BIRDS

Hummingbirds are the world's smallest birds. They are similar to many small passerines, but actually belong to the swift group, the apodiforms. Most species have very long, thin bills which they probe deep into flowers, to reach the sweet, energy-packed nectar. Their wings beat so fast that they allow the hummingbird to hover, and they also make the humming noise this bird is named after.

Ruby-throated hummingbird

THRUSHES AND WRENS

Thrushes, which include the American robin, are familiar in the garden. They eat a wide variety of foods, from worms, insects and other invertebrates, to shoots, seeds and fruits. Wrens are among the smallest of the group and flit, often unnoticed, in the undergrowth.

WALLCREEPER
Originally a bird of rocky uplands and cliffs, the wallcreeper now searches for insects on the walls of our buildings.

REDSTART
During courtship, the male redstart spreads out his brilliant russet-coloured tail feathers. This feature led to the bird's name, 'start' from the old word steort, meaning 'tail'.

Some of the groups of smaller perching birds:

Buntings
552 species

Warblers
339 species

Thrushes
304 species

Flycatchers
156 species

Finches
155 species

Larks, wagtails and pipits
130 species

Weavers
95 species

Swallows
74 species

Dippers and wrens
64 species

Tits
62 species

Sparrows
35 species

Nuthatches
21 species

Treecreepers
14 species

INSIDE A BIRD

A bird's body is highly adapted to save weight, for ease of flying. It is covered with lightweight feathers, and its bones are hollow. It also lacks teeth, which are relatively heavy, and has a beak made of the lightweight horny substance, keratin.

BREATHING

A bird's life is extremely active and flying uses up large amounts of energy and oxygen. To obtain this oxygen, the bird's respiratory or breathing system does not take air into the lungs and then breathe it out. The air flows in a more continuous one-way direction through the lungs, using a system of hollow bags called air sacs, in various parts of the upper body and also in the bones.

This helps to save weight and also makes the bird's lungs up to five times more efficient at taking in oxygen, than our own lungs.

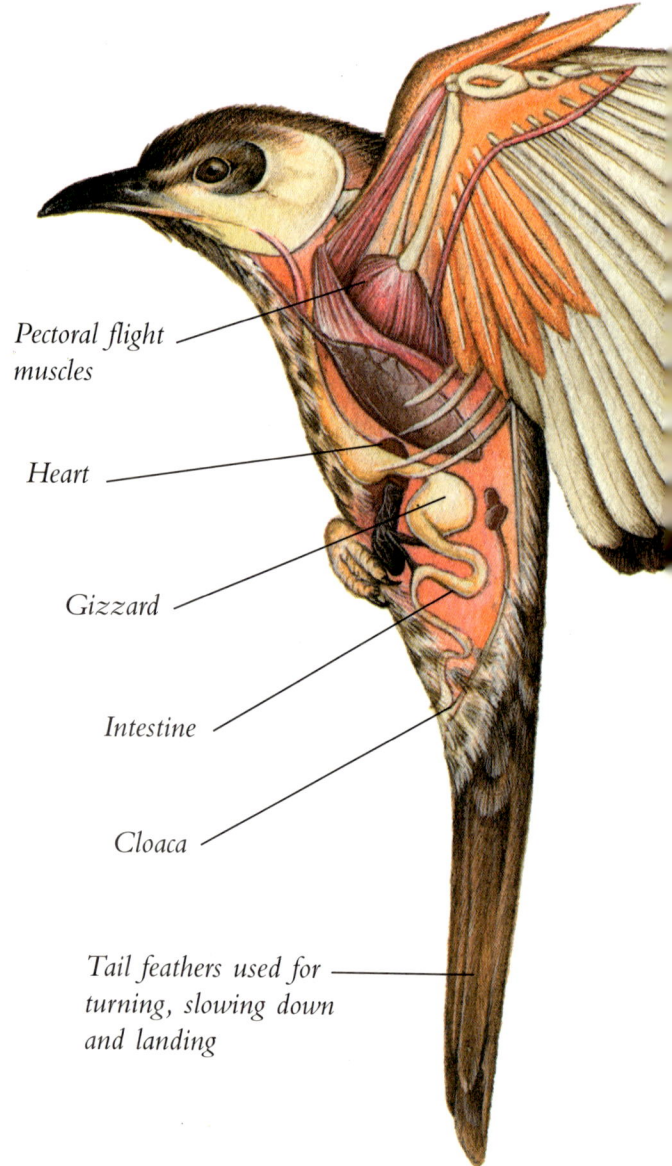

Pectoral flight muscles

Heart

Gizzard

Intestine

Cloaca

Tail feathers used for turning, slowing down and landing

32

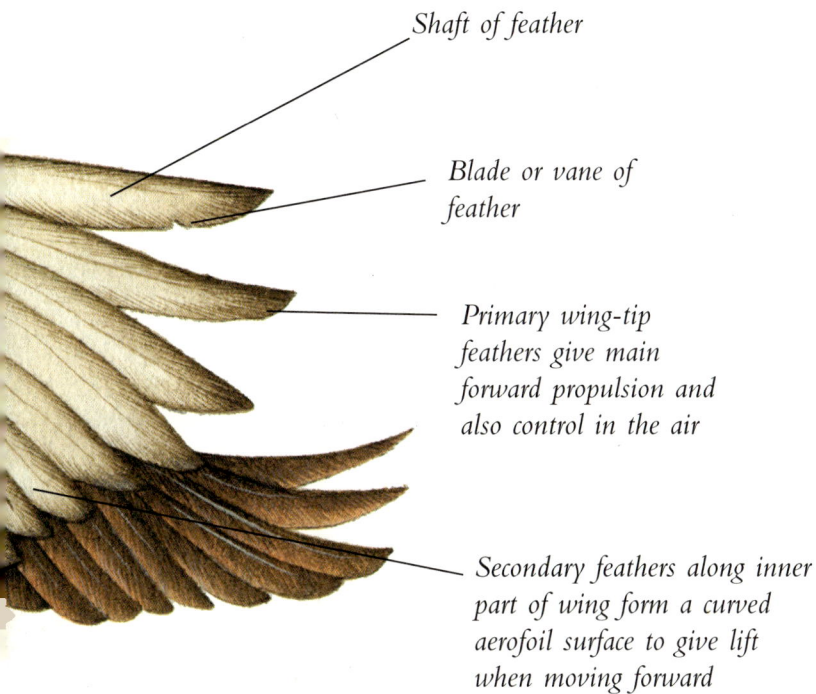

Shaft of feather

Blade or vane of
feather

Primary wing-tip
feathers give main
forward propulsion and
also control in the air

Secondary feathers along inner
part of wing form a curved
aerofoil surface to give lift
when moving forward

FEATHERS

A bird has two main kinds of feathers. The
contour feathers over its body and on its wings
have large, flat, blade-like surfaces. They give
protection, repel water and form an airtight
surface for flying. Under the contour feathers
on the body are soft, fluffy down feathers.
These form an air-trapping blanket to retain
body heat and keep the bird warm.

Parts of a bird's body:

- Cloaca - pouch that opens
  to the outside into which
  the gut, bladder and
  reproductive organs empty
  their products
- Gizzard - a part of the gut
  with muscular walls where
  food is mashed up or
  ground with stones
- Heart - muscular organ
  which pumps blood around
  the circulatory system
- Intestines - long tube where
  digested food and water is
  absorbed into the blood
  stream
- Lung – organ where
  inspired air is brought into
  close contact with blood for
  the exchange of respiratory
  gases oxygen and carbon
  dioxide
- Pectoral flight muscles –
  very strong muscles to help
  the bird lift its wings to take
  off and fly

SCAVENGING

All animals and plants die eventually, although some are very long-lived. What happens to all the dead bodies, and to all the droppings the animals produced during their lives, and to the leaves that drop from the trees? They become food for scavengers – animals and other living things which specialize in eating the corpses of other creatures.

THE VARIETY OF SCAVENGERS

Scavengers vary from majestic vultures and eagles, to beetles and crabs, to worms and maggots. They play a specialized role in ecology as detritivores, feeding on detritus – the mix of dead animals and plants and their products.

LIFE FROM DEATH
Vultures on the African plains jostle for position on the corpse. They strip the bones bare. Hyaenas and jackals also join the feast.

Microscopic organisms such as bacteria and fungi finish the job, gradually rotting and recycling even bones, teeth, horns, claws and other leftover hard parts, back into the soil to provide nutrients and minerals for new plant growth.

Common scavengers:

- Gulls such as herring and black-backed gulls are renowned scavengers, and can often be seen circling over rubbish tips where they will seek out any edible remains. They also feed on any dead animals they may come across.

- Crows often help to keep our roads clean by eating the remains of small mammals killed by traffic.

- Some flies lay their eggs on the bodies of dead animals. When the eggs hatch, the maggots feed on the flesh, helping to break it down.

- Other insects involved in waste disposal are the sexton beetles, which burrow beneath a corpse. They lay their eggs in a chamber dug from the soil nearby. When the larvae hatch they feed on the decaying flesh.

- Many kinds of dung beetle feed on animal dung and lay their eggs in it.

EGGS AND NESTS

The hard-shelled eggs which birds lay are a splendid adaptation to life on land, even in dry and desert conditions. However, eggs are vulnerable to certain predators and must therefore be protected – either by the adult birds, or by being concealed in a nest.

Many eggs are laid in the open. But they are patterned to match their background, with irregular blotches or squiggles.

Various seabirds find safety in numbers, and also by choosing nest sites that are difficult for predators to reach, such as sea cliffs or isolated islands.

INCUBATION

Birds must incubate their eggs, which means keeping them warm enough in cold conditions so that the embryos (babies) can develop inside. In hot climates, the parent birds often have the

AWKWARD ACCESS

Weaver birds, such as the red-headed weaver, build their nests from stems, leaves, moss, grass and thorns woven together into a strong structure. The nest is suspended from a branch tip and its opening faces down, so it is difficult for predators to enter.

36

NESTING TOGETHER

Village weaver birds build their nests woven together into a colonial structure, which may be five metres across. If a predator tries to steal the eggs, all members of the group squawk alarm calls and flap nearby. These noisy birds live in Africa, in a variety of habitats including farmland and parks.

opposite problem. They must prevent the eggs overheating, by shielding them from the direct sun, or even by wetting them from their own breast feathers.

Incubation times vary from species to species, from about 10 days in small songbirds to as long as 80 days in albatrosses.

HELPLESS OR ABLE?

The young of many birds, such as thrushes and other songbirds, are naked and helpless for the first couple of weeks. They must be tended and fed by their parents.

In others, for example gamebirds, waterfowl and shorebirds, the chicks have feathers and can run and even fend for themselves soon after hatching.

Egg and nest records:

• The largest egg is that of the ostrich. It can be 20 centimetres long and weigh up to two kilograms.

• The largest egg relative to body size is laid by the kiwi. It may be almost one-quarter of the mother's body weight.

• The smallest eggs are laid by hummingbirds, and may be less than 10 millimetres in length and weigh only one-third of one gram.

• Hummingbirds also make tiny nests – thimble-shaped cups woven partly from spiders' webs.

• Some birds, such as the fairy tern, make no nest at all. This tropical seabird balances its egg on a bare tree branch, hoping for calm weather.

• The largest single nests are made by eagles over many years. They can be three metres across.

FISH

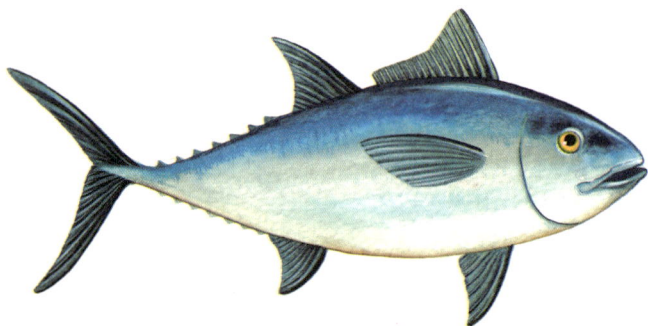

Fish form the largest of all the vertebrate groups (animals with backbones). There are more than 25,000 species known. They live wherever there is water from cold mountain streams to warm tropical lakes, and in all the oceans of the world, from at (and sometimes above) the surface to the greatest depths. Fish have many adaptations to their aquatic life. These include a streamlined body shape with fins to aid swimming, and gills to breathe dissolved oxygen

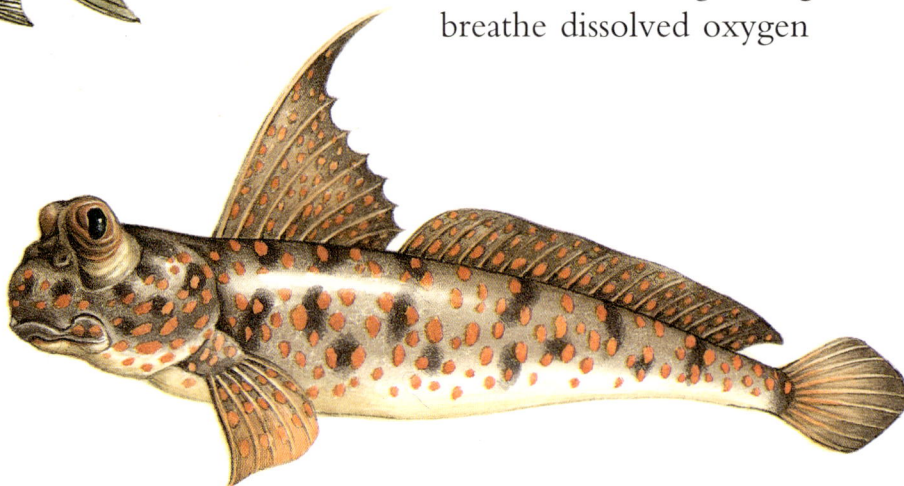

from the water. The gills are feathery, and
contain many thin-walled blood vessels
which take up oxygen as the water
passes through them. The bodies
of most fish are covered by
scales which overlap each
other and form a very
smooth, flexible surface.
These scales protect the fish,
but also allow them to bend and
slither easily through the water.

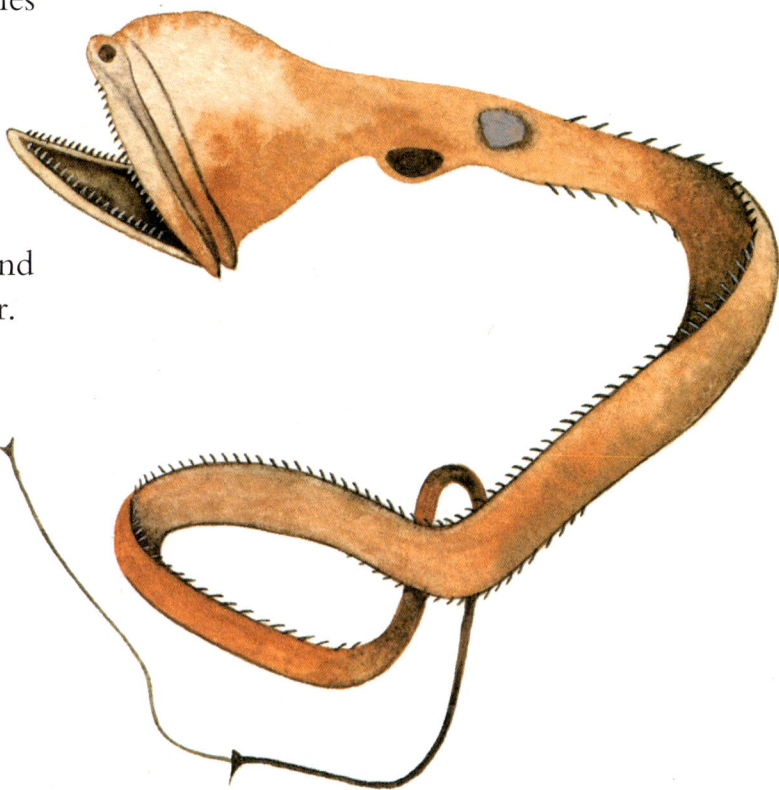

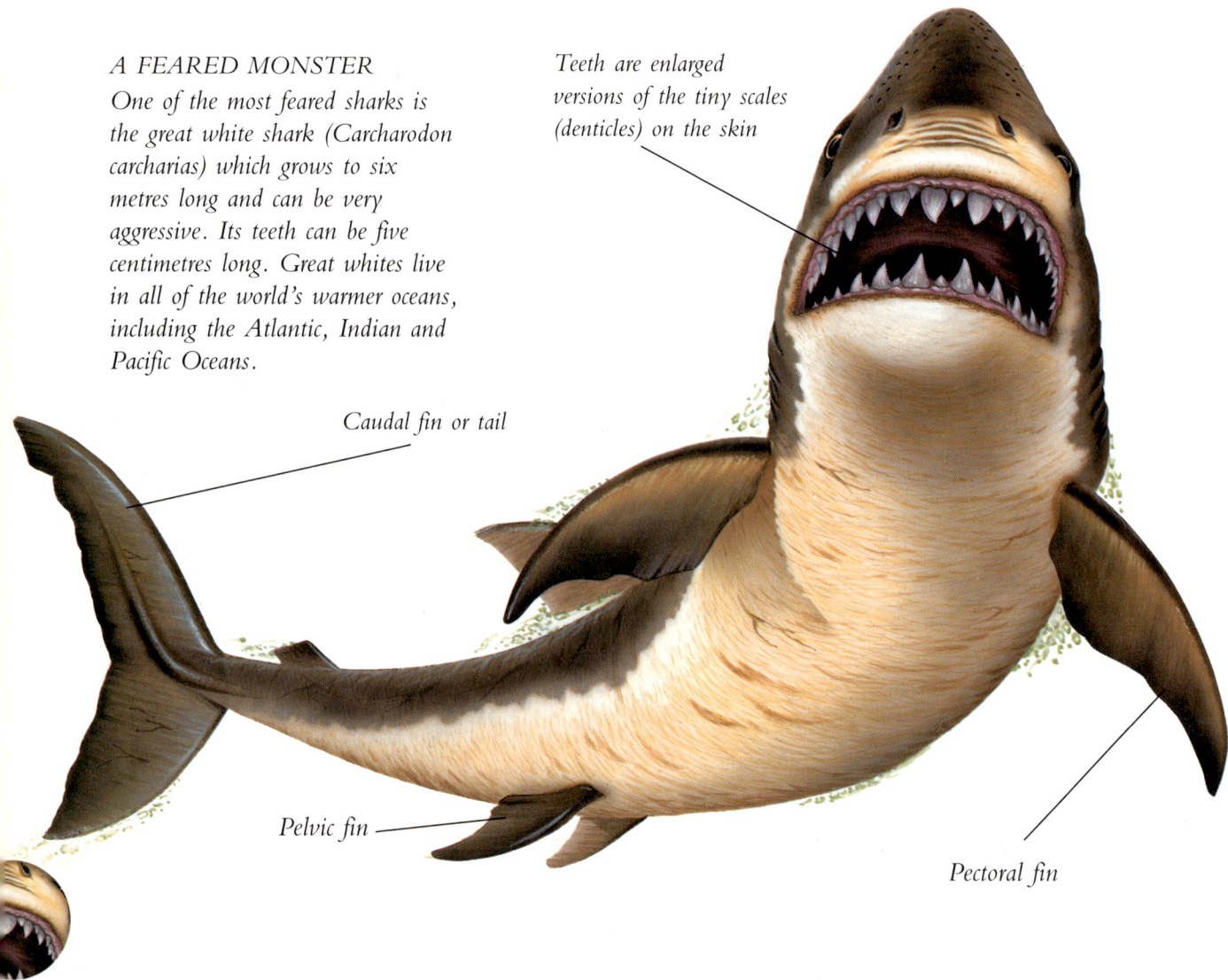

SHARKS AND RAYS

A FEARED MONSTER

One of the most feared sharks is the great white shark (Carcharodon carcharias) which grows to six metres long and can be very aggressive. Its teeth can be five centimetres long. Great whites live in all of the world's warmer oceans, including the Atlantic, Indian and Pacific Oceans.

Teeth are enlarged versions of the tiny scales (denticles) on the skin

Caudal fin or tail

Pelvic fin

Pectoral fin

The majority of fish have skeletons made of bones. But the cartilaginous fish have skeletons made of cartilage or gristle. The best known are the sharks. Most are large, fierce predators that use their sharp triangular teeth to kill other animals and tear their flesh. Only a few of the larger sharks are dangerous to humans, but many people are attacked each year, mainly in tropical waters. Dogfish are small, harmless types of sharks.

SKATES AND RAYS

These are like sharks which have been rolled flat! Their side or pectoral fins form large 'wings' for flying through the water. Stingrays have sharp spines along their tails and some can deliver a poisonous sting. Rays and skates often spend long periods resting on the seabed, where they can be difficult to spot – until they move. They eat mainly shellfish, crabs, worms and similar animals buried in the sand and mud.

Cartilaginous fish (Chondrichthyes)

710 species
- cartilage skeleton
- rough scales
- most have sharp teeth
- fins are less flexible than those of other fish

Two main subgroups:

Sharks (Selachii)

370 species
- long and streamlined
- most are active hunters
- all live in the sea

Skates and rays (Batoidea)

340 species
- flattened body with side 'wings'
- swim by rippling or flapping their wings
- many eat shellfish or worms in the mud

POND AND LAKE FISH

Most lakes support good populations of fish, unless they are very poor in nutrients, or very badly polluted. Typical pond and lake fish of temperate regions are carp, loach, tench, perch and brown trout. Fish such as carp and tench, which grub about on the muddy pond floor, have small eyes and feelers (barbels) near their mouths, to help them find food.

EVOLUTION IN ACTION

The fish of the East African lakes are world famous, mainly because there are so many closely related species. Lake Victoria (bordered by Uganda, Kenya and Tanzania) has over 170 species of cichlid fish, *Haplochromis*. Although they all live in the same lake, the different species tend to eat different prey. Some eat smaller fish and insects, while others browse

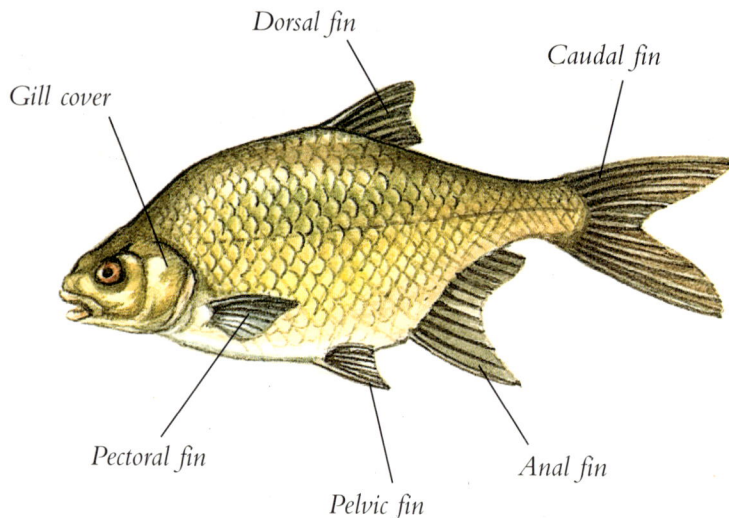

Dorsal fin

Caudal fin

Gill cover

Pectoral fin

Pelvic fin

Anal fin

PERCH

The perch shows clearly the various body parts of a typical bony fish. The pectoral and pelvic fins are paired, one of each pair on each side of the body. The dorsal, anal and caudal fins are unpaired. In bony fish the gills are protected under a bony flap on the side of the head, the gill-cover or operculum.

42

on algae. All of these fish probably evolved from one or a few common ancestors. Over millions of years the lake in which they all first lived shrank into several smaller lakes, which then expanded and merged again. These changing conditions led to the evolution of new and different species, each specializing on different food, but all with similar body features.

PIKE
The pike is an ambusher. It prefers weedy ponds and lakes, also reservoirs and slow-flowing rivers all around the Northern Hemisphere. It lurks in water plants and dashes out to grab victims with its huge mouth.

More groups of fish:

Jawless fish (Agnatha)
70 species
• simple cartilage skeleton
• no jaws
• no scales
• no proper fins
• many pairs of gills
• includes lampreys and hagfish

Lungfish (Choanichthyes)
6 species
• leg-like fleshy fins
• lungs as well as gills
• survive dry periods by burying into lake-bed mud

Bony fish (Osteichthyes)
24,500 species
• the main fish group
• bone skeleton
• smooth scales
• live in all watery habitats

RIVER FISH

Fish such as trout and salmon spend some of their lives in fast-flowing rivers. These fish must swim constantly to maintain their position in the river, or to make progress upstream. They have very muscular and flexible bodies and can even leap over small weirs or waterfalls.

Slower-moving rivers in temperate regions are home to fish such as chub, dace and roach. Barbel and gudgeon are also river fish. Tropical streams and rivers are home to hundreds of fish species. Many attractive freshwater tropical fish bred for aquaria, such as the bright iridescent red-and-blue neon tetra, come from the Amazon region of South America.

GAR PIKE
Slim and streamlined, the several kinds of gars feed by slashing at smaller fish with their long snout.

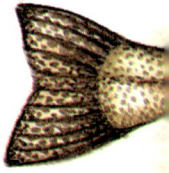

FOOD FISH

Some river fish, such as the rainbow trout, are bred specially for food. This species came originally from western North America, but as a result of fish farming it has now spread to most parts of the world.

PIRANHA

The typical piranha is quite small, rarely growing larger than a human hand. One or two piranha on their own are unlikely to attack large animals. But as soon as a shoal senses blood in the water, the fish attack in a feeding frenzy.

AN INFAMOUS FISH

Another famous, or rather infamous, Amazon river fish is the piranha (*Serrasalmus*). Piranhas have sharp teeth and hunt in big shoals or packs. Working together, they can strip the flesh from creatures which fall into the river. Some kinds of piranha are vegetarian, however, feeding on nuts and fruit.

Fish records

Smallest fish
The tiny Philippine Goby (*Pandaka pygmaea*) at 12 millimetres total length.

Biggest fish
The enormous whale shark (*Rhincodon typus*) at 15 metres long. Like all sharks, this is a cartilaginous fish.

Biggest bony fish
Probably the beluga (*Huso huso*), a kind of sturgeon found in the Caspian Sea, which reaches 8.5 metres in length. Another very big bony fish is the South American arapaima (Arapaima gigas), which grows to 4.5 metres.

Fastest fish
The sailfish, swordfish and mako shark have all been timed at over 80 kilometres per hour.

45

SEASHORE AND REEF FISH

The fish of coastal habitats must cope with ever-changing conditions. Tides rise and fall, waves batter the shore, fresh water (as rain) dilutes salt water, and small rock pools can ice over in winter or become as warm as a bath in summer.

CLINGING ON FOR LIFE
Gobies and blennies are common fish of rocky shores in temperate seas.

They cling on tight with their spiny fins or hide in crevices when the waves break. Mudskippers are common in mangrove swamps in West Africa, Southeast Asia and Australia. They spend much of their time partly submerged in mud or shallow water, but they can climb out into the air – and even clamber up mangrove stems using their arm-like fins.

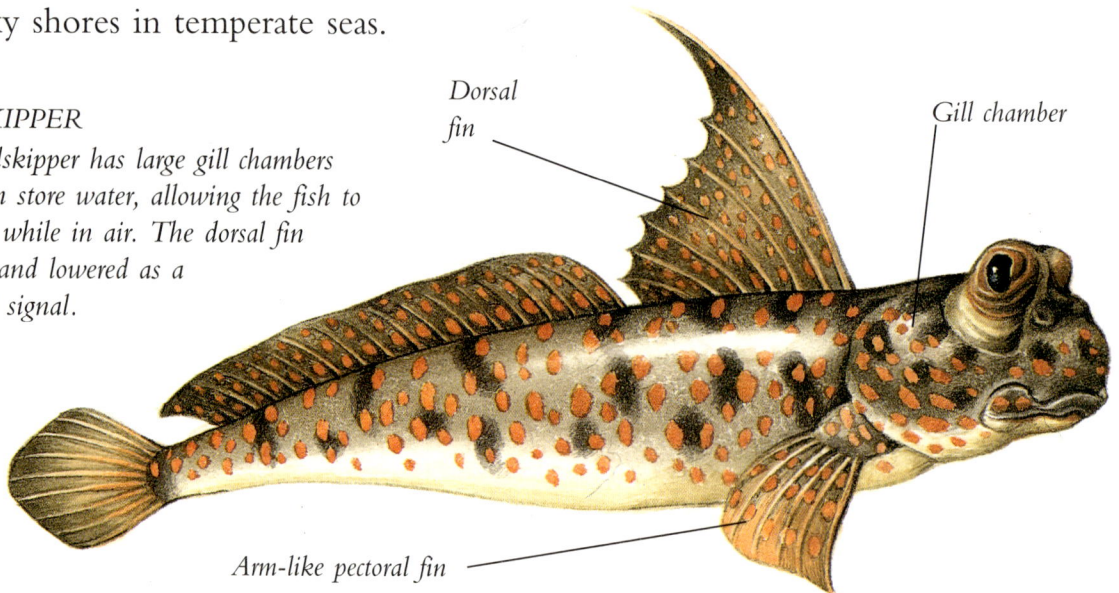

MUDSKIPPER
The mudskipper has large gill chambers which can store water, allowing the fish to 'breathe' while in air. The dorsal fin is raised and lowered as a territorial signal.

Dorsal fin

Gill chamber

Arm-like pectoral fin

ON THE REEF

Coral reef communities teem with shoals of brightly coloured fish. They use the many crevices in the coral rocks to hide from predators. One of the most remarkable of all tropical marine fish is the seahorse, named from its resemblance to a tiny horse. Some species have tasselled fins, making them blend into the background of frilly seaweeds and corals.

PUFFERFISH
By swallowing water, this fish becomes too big for other fish to swallow.

SHOALING
Small fish dart and turn together in a vast shoal, making it difficult for a predator to single out a victim.

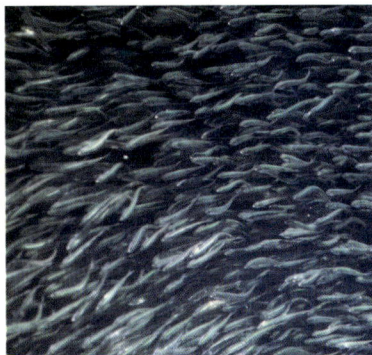

Fish of the seashore
Gobies
Blennies
Wrasses
Butterfish
Mudskippers

Coral reef fish
Parrotfish
Groupers
Clownfish
Moorish idols
Seahorses
Stonefish

Fascinating fish
• Some clownfish live among the stinging tentacles of sea anemones. The fish themselves are protected by a special layer of body slime or mucus. Any other kind of fish risks being stung to death and eaten by the anemone.
• The stonefish is one of the world's most poisonous fish. It has sharp spines which can inject a deadly venom.

OCEAN FISH

Many fish live in the open sea. Some are adapted to life near the surface. Here, where the sunlight penetrates, there is plenty of food, from tiny algae and microscopic plankton, through to shrimps, squid and baby fish. Surface-dwelling ocean fish tend to be fast swimmers with keen eyesight, such as mackerel, tuna and marlin.

THE BOTTOM OF THE WORLD

The depths of the ocean are cold and dark, but the mud of the ocean floor offers rich pickings of worms and other food. Deep-sea fish include the bizarre gulper eel and the

MARLIN
This sleek billfish folds its fins against its body and goes at full speed as it thrashes its tail.

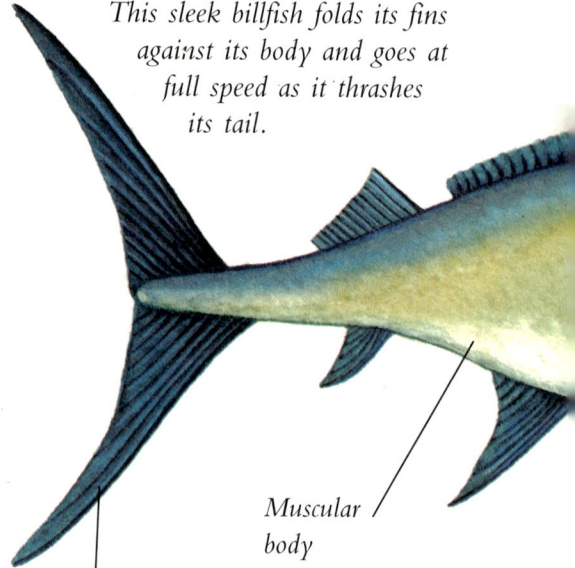

Muscular body

Crescent-shaped tail for fast swimming

BLUE-FIN TUNA
The tuna or tunny hunts smaller fish and squid. It is itself hunted by larger fish such as mako and tiger sharks, as well as our own fishing fleets.

equally peculiar anglerfish. Some, like the hatchet fish and lanternfish, produce their own light in this pitch-dark, cold habitat. Since meals tend to be few and far between, many deep-sea fish have huge mouths to swallow the occasional large prey.

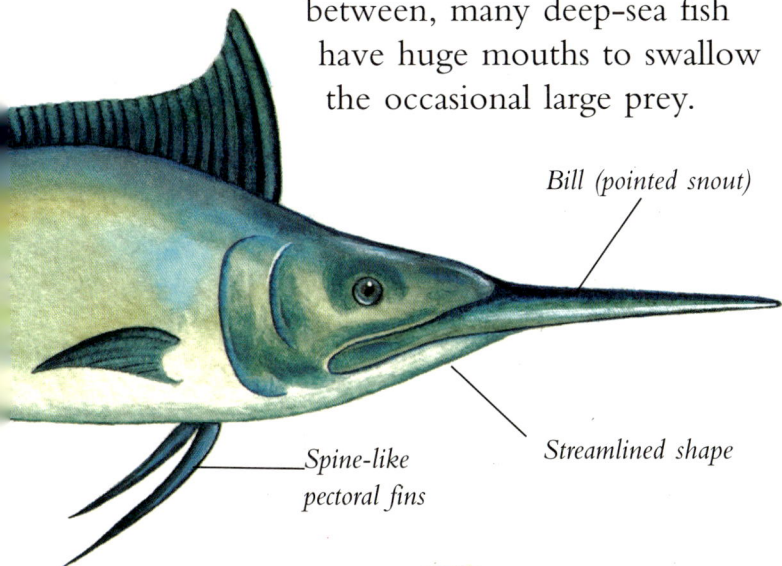

Bill (pointed snout)

Streamlined shape

Spine-like pectoral fins

GULPER EEL
This fish is little more than a vast mouth and flexible, bag-like stomach. When hungry, its body is thin and eel-like. It expands enormously with each meal.

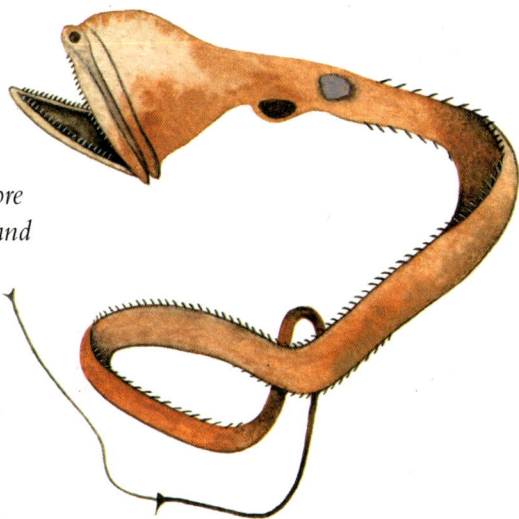

Fish of the upper ocean
Marlin
Swordfish
Tuna
Mackerel
Herring
Flying fish
Wolf-fish
Ocean sunfish
Plaice

Fish of the deep ocean
Halibut
Gulper eel
Anglerfish
Ribbonfish
Tripod fish
Hatchet fish

Fish in mid air
• Flying fish can leap as high as 6 metres above the sea's surface, then use their wing-like fins to glide for up to 300 metres. They are found mainly in tropical seas.

INSIDE A FISH

A fish's body is mostly muscles, arranged in a zig-zag pattern along the sides of the vertebral column, or backbone. The digestive, reproductive and other organs are packed into the lower one-third of the body. Most fish have a swim bladder, which can be filled with bubbles of gas to help the fish rise or float still in the water. However, sharks and rays lack a swim bladder. They must keep swimming to stay in mid-water.

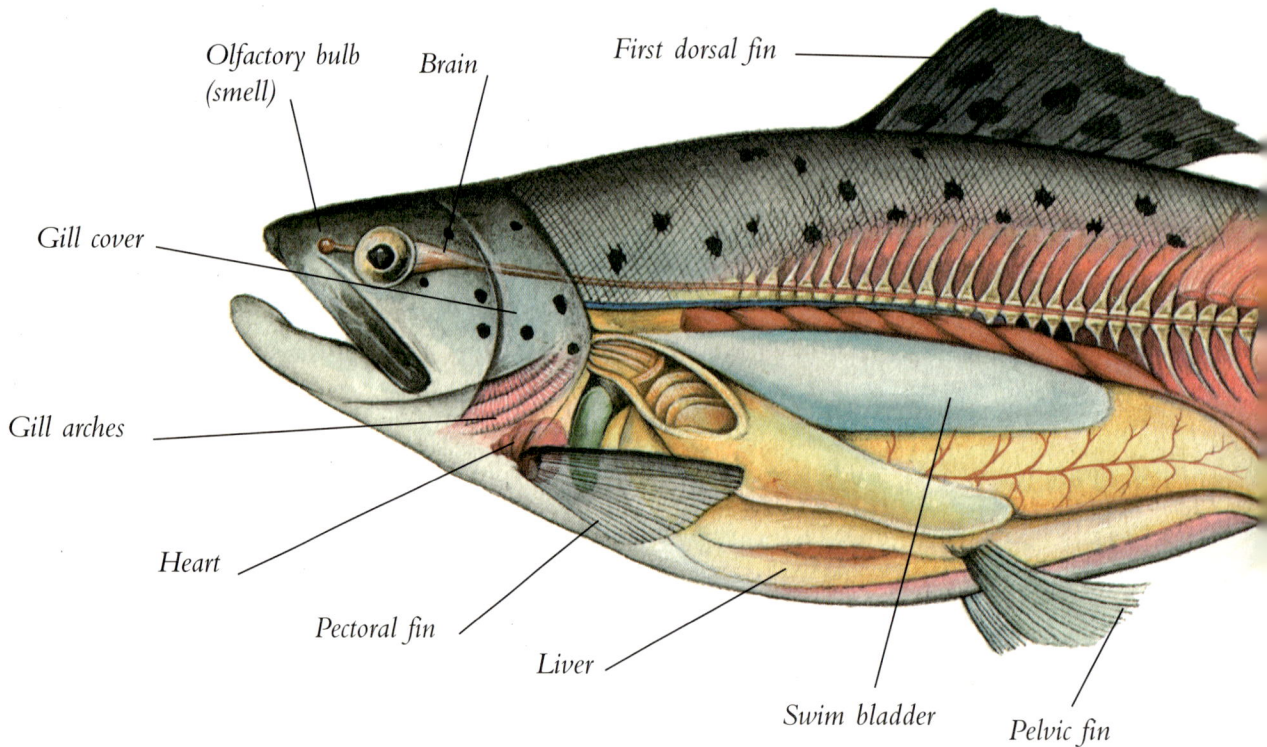

Olfactory bulb (smell)

Brain

First dorsal fin

Gill cover

Gill arches

Heart

Pectoral fin

Liver

Swim bladder

Pelvic fin

BLOCKS OF MUSCLE

The fish's muscles are arranged in blocks, called myotomes. This is an evolutionary leftover from the ancient ancestors of fish, which had body segments, like worms. The individual bones of the spinal column have long rod-like extensions for anchoring these muscles. The myotomes pull on each side alternately, bending the backbone to make the tail swish and propel the fish forwards.

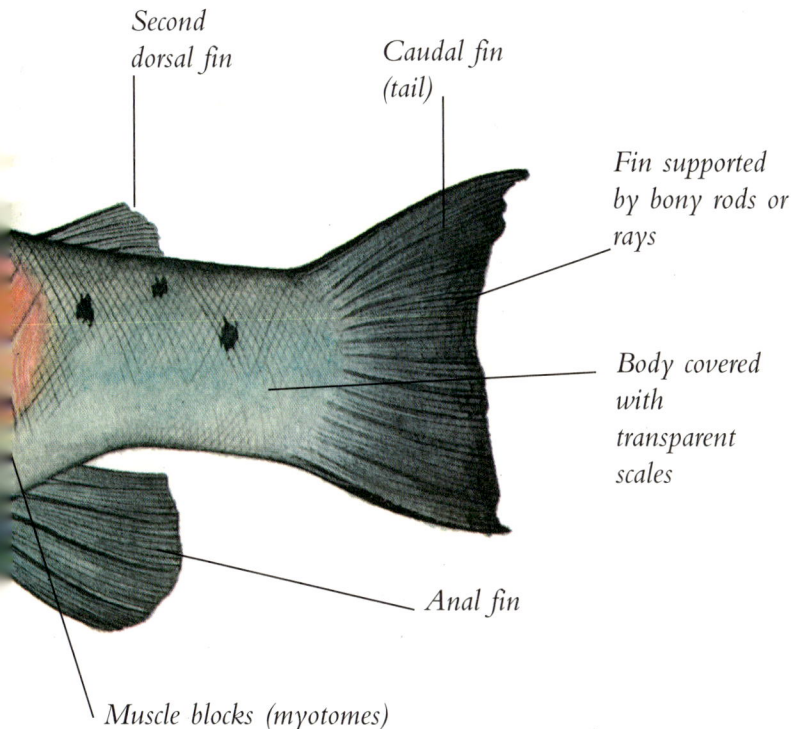

Second dorsal fin

Caudal fin (tail)

Fin supported by bony rods or rays

Body covered with transparent scales

Anal fin

Muscle blocks (myotomes)

Parts of a fish's body

- Alimentary canal – the gut or digestive tube between the mouth and anus
- Brain - organ in the head where sensory nerve messages are received and sorted and motor messages sent out to the muscles in response
- Gills – respiratory organs of aquatic animals where blood vessels are brought close to the skin surface
- Heart - muscular organ which pumps blood around the circulatory system
- Liver - organ which processes digested food and regulates body chemistry
- Operculum - the bony flap which covers the opening to the gills in fish
- Swim bladder - this is a bag of air inside fishes bodies. It makes them lighter so they can float as well as swim.

51

EXTINCTION OF WILDLIFE

Throughout the long history of life on Earth, species have become extinct. It is a natural part of evolution by natural selection. Scientists estimate that over 99 per cent of all the species of animals which have ever lived have become extinct. The main evidence for them is fossils. They include a host of invertebrates, such as trilobites, as well as more impressive creatures such as the dinosaurs.

SYMBOL OF EXTINCTION
The dodo was a turkey-sized flightless pigeon from the Indian Ocean island of Mauritius. Inoffensive, and a useful source of fresh meat for passing sailors, it became extinct at the end of the 17th century.

FASTER AND FASTER
In recent decades, the activities of people have caused an increasing number of animal and plant extinctions, and much of our wildlife is today threatened as never before. Animals which evolved on isolated oceanic islands have been particularly vulnerable. Most live nowhere else, and cannot be relocated because they are so closely adapted to their unique island habitat. Many have been driven to extinction by introduced predators such as cats and rats. Others suffer at the development of tropical 'paradise islands', as the natural vegetation is cleared for the tourist and leisure business.

EXTINCT OR NOT?

When is an animal truly extinct? The Tasmanian wolf, also called the Tasmanian tiger or thylacine, was a dog-like mammal from Tasmania, south of mainland Australia. The last known individual died as a captive in the zoo at Hobart, the Tasmanian capital, in 1936.

The species is now presumed extinct. But occasional claimed sightings persist. Some experts believe the thylacine lurks in the dense Tasmanian forests and, like the coelacanth of African waters, waits to be rediscovered.

NEVER SAY DIE?

The coelacanth is an unusual fish with a fleshy lobe at the base of each fin. Its fossils are known from the time of the dinosaurs, but then it seemed to die out – until 1938, when a coelacanth was caught off the east coast of Africa. The fish was known to local fishermen, but scientists were amazed. Since then several more have been caught and studied.

Examples of some animal extinctions:

Moa

The moas of New Zealand were flightless birds taller than a human, resembling giant kiwis. They were hunted to extinction by the early human settlers, finally dying out around 1800.

Great auk

This flightless relative of guillemots went extinct in 1844 when the last known bird was killed near Iceland.

Quagga

This zebra-relative from South Africa was hunted to extinction in the 1880s.

Passenger pigeon

This pigeon used to occur in huge numbers in North America, turning the sky black for hours in its gigantic flocks. But it was hunted to extinction in the wild by about 1900.

HABITAT DESTRUCTION

The destruction of habitats is the greatest of all threats to wildlife, be they rich tropical forests, mangrove swamps, coral reefs, or your own local grassland or wood. Most wild plants and animals are so closely adapted to their own particular habitat that they become rare or endangered if this is damaged or removed.

MORE HABITAT

The paradise whydah is a bird of dry open country in Africa. As farmland spreads at the expense of forests, its habitat is actually becoming larger. However, the male is hunted for its spectacular tail feathers.

MOST AT RISK

Globally, the most worrying losses of habitat are the tropical rainforests, because these contain by far the largest number of species. Although large areas of tropical forest still survive, they are still being lost at an alarming rate – hundreds of thousands of square kilometres each year.

Coral reefs, another rich habitat, are threatened by overfishing and shell collection. But perhaps a greater threat is the mud and silt from land erosion, which enters the shallow-sea coral area from nearby rivers, and kills the live corals.

LOGGED AND GONE

After an area of tropical forest is logged and cleared, it takes at least a century to regrow.

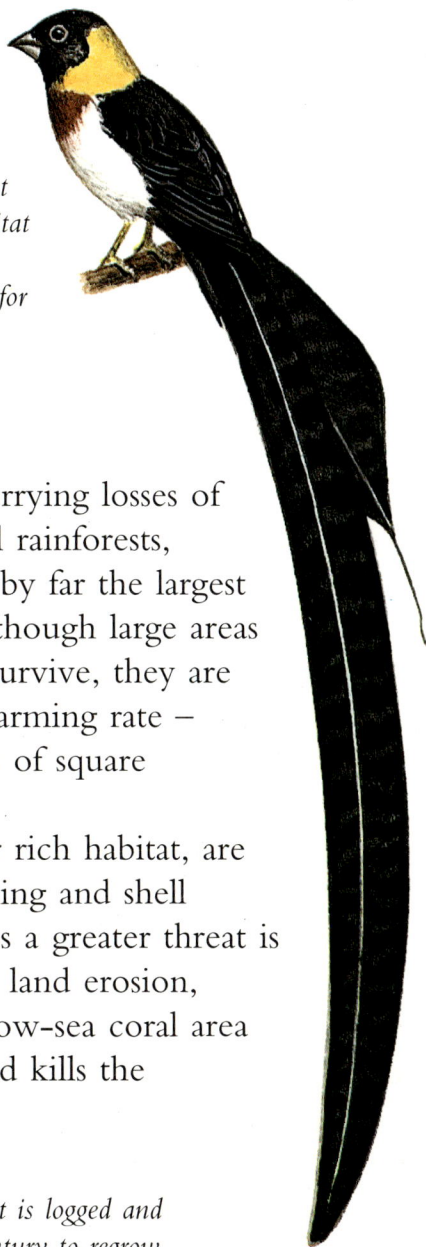

More threatened habitats:

Wetlands

• Marshes, swamps and other wetlands everywhere are very vulnerable to pollution of the waterways which sustain them. Their plants and animals are easily poisoned.

• Many wetlands are viewed more as 'wastelands'. They are drained to provide more and more land for growing crops.

Mangrove swamps

• These coastal subtropical and tropical areas of mangrove trees are under threat in many places, especially in Southeast Asia, where they are often converted to rice paddies.

• But when the mangroves have been removed, the coast becomes much more vulnerable to erosion by storms.

POLLUTION

Pollution comes from many different sources: chemicals draining from farmland, factories or sewage outflows; fumes pouring from vehicles, factories and power stations; and events such as leaks from oil pipelines or tankers at sea.

ACID RAIN
Every year pollution kills countless numbers of wild animals and plants. It

CHEMICALS IN THE WATER
The valuable metal gold is sometimes extracted from rivers using the poisonous metal mercury. The mercury washes downstream with devastating results, killing fish and plants.

can even affect nature reserves and other wildlife refuges. A particular problem is caused by acid rain. Rain becomes unnaturally acid when it absorbs sulphur and nitrogen, which

RISING SEAS
Global warming was detected in the late 1990s by climate experts. As the polar ice caps melt, sea levels could flood millions of square kilometres of low-lying land. This would destroy valuable wildlife habitats such as coastal marshes and mangrove swamps – and also hundreds of ports and coastal towns.

are put into the air mainly from the burning of coal, gas and oil, used as fuel for cars, factories, houses and power stations. This acid rain reduces the fertility of the soil and causes damages trees and water life.

Acid rain usually falls hundreds of kilometres away from the polluting area. It is an international problem and has already damaged huge tracts of forests in northern North America, Europe and northern Asia.

Pollution high in the sky:

- In recent years scientists have found that several chemicals have damaged the upper atmosphere, with far-reaching effects.

- The upper atmosphere contains a layer with high levels of a gas called ozone. When this gas forms at low levels it can cause illnesses such as asthma.

- But the natural ozone layer of the upper atmosphere protects the Earth from the harmful ultraviolet (UV) radiation from the Sun.

- Scientists have found that there is a thinning or hole in the normally complete ozone layer. This is growing, damaged by several different chemical pollutants.

- International agreements have limited the production of some ozone-destroying chemicals. But the problem will persist for many years to come.

PESTS

When species are brought or introduced to new areas, either deliberately or by accident, they may upset the delicate ecological balance. This can have devastating results. Introduced species can quickly become animal pests or plant weeds, out-competing the native animals or plants and causing local extinctions. Such pests can then be extremely difficult to eradicate or control.

Introduced predators include cats, rats, weasels, pigs and mongooses. They have especially severe effects on small islands where the ecology is already fragile. Goats, deer, pigs and rabbits are commonly introduced and

RATS AND RABBITS

Rats are supreme survivors. They thrive on the same foods we do, whether these are growing in the fields, stored after harvest, or thrown away as leftovers. Rabbits hide in their burrows, eat our crops or grazing grassland, and breed so rapidly that they have spread to every continent except Antarctica.

BIOLOGICAL CONTROL

The prickly-pear cactus, originally from North America, was introduced to Australia where it soon become a weed. However it has been partly controlled by another introduced species, a moth from Argentina, whose caterpillars eat the cactus.

have had dramatic impact on islands with no native browsing herbivores, such as in New Zealand and Hawaii.

OUT OF CONTROL

Some weed or pest species, such as rats and mice, and plants such as plantains and pineapple weed, have managed to spread themselves around the globe without special help from people. Despite precautions, they manage to evade our controls.

As genetically-modified crops and farm animals begin to appear, will they also escape and become established in the wild, adding to the chaos?

An infamous weed – the water hyacinth:

- One of the most notorious of all introduced weeds, this is a floating lily-like plant from tropical America.

- Its large leaves and attractive purple flowers have choked waterways in many countries, becoming a very serious nuisance.

- Water hyacinth has spread to the southern USA, Africa, Australia, India, Sri Lanka, Malaya, and even to Tahiti and the Solomon Islands. In many places it has altered the ecology and impeded boat traffic, especially clogging boat propellers.

- In just three years it choked some 1,500 kilometres of the Zaire River.

- As it dies and rots, water hyacinth uses up valuable dissolved oxygen in the water, killing animals such as fish.

59

PARKS AND SANCTUARIES

Wildlife reserves, national parks and sanctuaries of various kinds have been established throughout the world, to try and preserve as much of our wildlife heritage as possible. Some seek to exclude people, while others try and involve local people, especially where traditional use of the habitat combines with conservation.

ECO-TOURISM

In most cases the reserves may be visited by naturalists and tourists. But there are usually restrictions to protect the wildlife. Eco-tourism, where income from visitors helps conservation projects, is a fast-growing business.

BLACK-FOOTED FERRET
Prairie dogs are the main food of this agile carnivore. But prairie dogs are also pests, and often poisoned. The poison accumulates in the ferret's body and causes illness and death.

PLATYPUS
River pollution has affected the worms, shellfish and other foods of this unique Australian monotreme (egg-laying mammal).

The Everglades, a huge swamp at the tip of Florida, USA, is a famous wildlife reserve. It is fed by fresh water seeping through it from a lake and river. The water forms pools, marshes and meandering channels – it is one of the greatest wildlife sites in the world. The heart of this ecosystem is protected by the Everglades National Park, a Biosphere Reserve and World Heritage Site covering 566,000 hectares.

EVERGLADES INHABITANTS

The Everglades is home to rare species such as the wood stork, Everglades kite, reddish egret and the endangered Florida 'panther', a local version of the puma (cougar or mountain lion).

SNAIL FOOD
The Everglades kite is a local form of the snail kite of Central and South America. It feeds almost entirely on one kind of water snail, extracting the flesh using its specially adapted narrow, curved bill.

Some notable wildlife parks and marine sanctuaries:

Baikal, Russia
- The world's deepest lake, and over 25 million years old. It contains about 960 species of animal and 400 species of plants found nowhere else in the world.

Fjordland National Park, New Zealand
- Unspoilt forest and hills, and home to rare birds such as the takahe and kakapo.

Galapagos National Park, Ecuador
- Made famous by naturalist Charles Darwin, the island inhabitants include Darwin's finches, giant tortoises and marine iguanas.

Great Barrier Reef, Australia
- This vast coastal and underwater reserve protects the world's greatest coral reefs.

INDEX

ACKNOWLEDGEMENTS

The publishers wish to thank the following artists who have
contributed to this book.

David Ashby, Mike Atkinson, Wayne Ford, Roger Kent,
Stuart Lafford (Linden Artists),Alan Male (Linden Artists),
Terry Riley.

All photographs from the Miles Kelly Archive.